Mein erstes Bildwörterbuch Englisch

Illustrationen von Kim Woolley

Inhalt

Haustiere	2	Zu Hause	16
Insekten	3	Meine Familie	18
Im Tierpark	4	Kindergeburtstag	19
Auf dem Bauernhof	5	Mein Körper	20
Sport und Spiel	6	Beim Arzt	21
Auf dem Jahrmarkt	7	Kleidung	22
Am Strand	8	Spielzeug	23
Gebäude	10	In der Schule	24
Verkehr	11	Formen und Farben	26
In der Stadt	12	Märchen und Sagen	27
Im Supermarkt	14	Unsere Erde	28
Kochen und Backen	15	Wörterverzeichnis von A – Z	29

Alle Tätigkeitswörter (Verben) sind im Unterschied zu den Hauptwörtern (Substantiven) grau gedruckt.

Delphin Verlag

Haustiere

Insekten

Im Tierpark

Auf dem Bauernhof

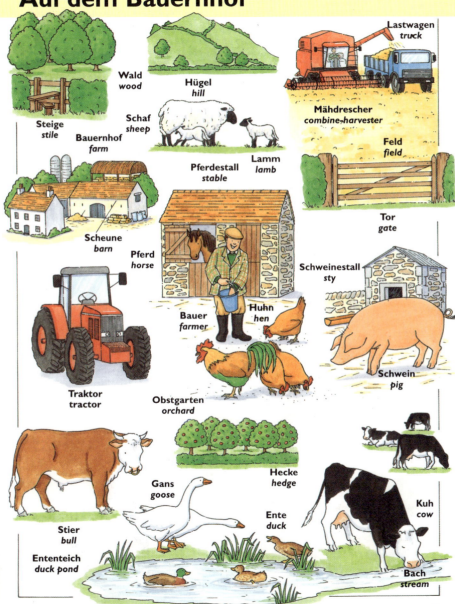

Gebäude

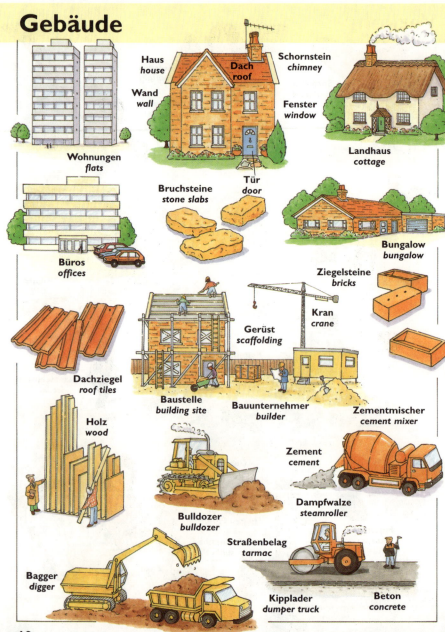

In der Stadt

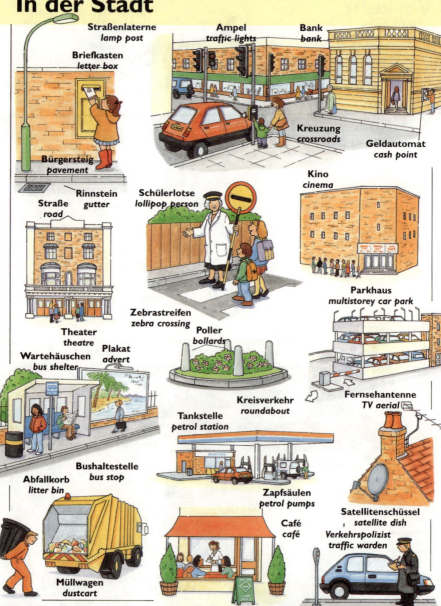

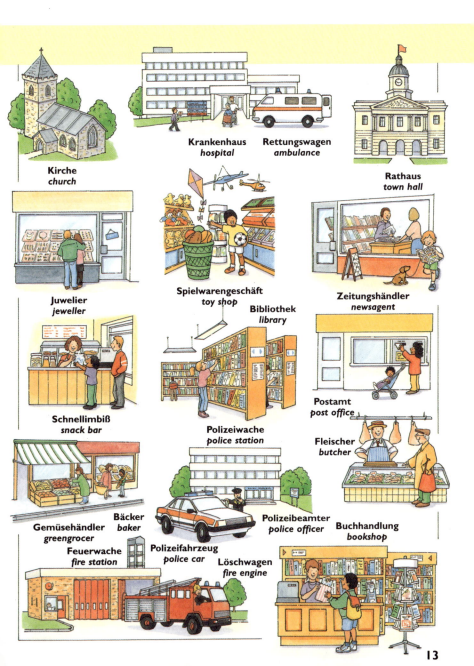

Im Supermarkt

Kochen und Backen

Zu Hause

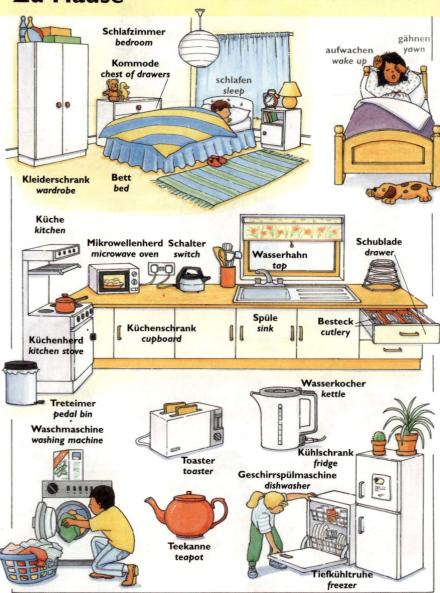

Meine Familie

jung / *young*   **jünger** / *younger*   **am jüngsten** / *youngest*

alt / *old*   **älter** / *older*   **am ältesten** / *oldest*

Mama / *mummy*

Papa / *daddy*

Schwester / *sister*

Bruder / *brother*

Eltern / *parents*

Sohn / *son*

Tochter / *daughter*

Onkel / *uncle*

Tante / *aunt*

Neffe / *nephew*

Nichte / *niece*

Cousin / *cousin*

Oma / *granny*

Opa / *grandpa*

Enkel / *grandchild*

Zwillinge / *twins*

Baby / *baby*

Drillinge / *triplets*

Mein Körper

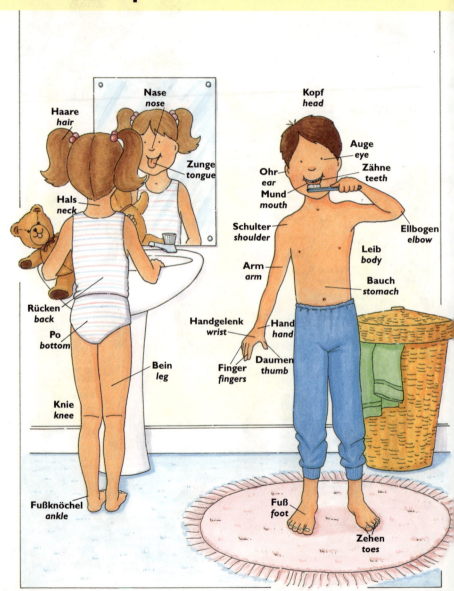

Beim Arzt

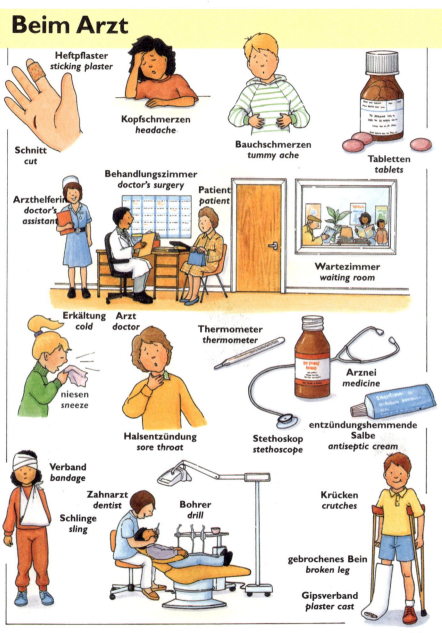

Kleidung

T-Shirt *T-shirt*

Pullover *pullover*

Hut *hat*

ausziehen *undress*

Shorts *shorts*

Jeans *jeans*

Baseballmütze *baseball cap*

Sweatshirt *sweatshirt*

Pantoffeln *slippers*

Kapuze *hood*

Schal *scarf*

Anorak *anorak*

Handschuh *glove*

Hemd *shirt*

Hose *trousers*

Rock *skirt*

Gummistiefel *rubber boots*

Strumpfhose *tights*

anziehen *dress*

Unterhemd *vest*

Unterhose *pants*

Strickjacke *cardigan*

Turnschuhe *trainers*

Kleid *dress*

Strümpfe *socks*

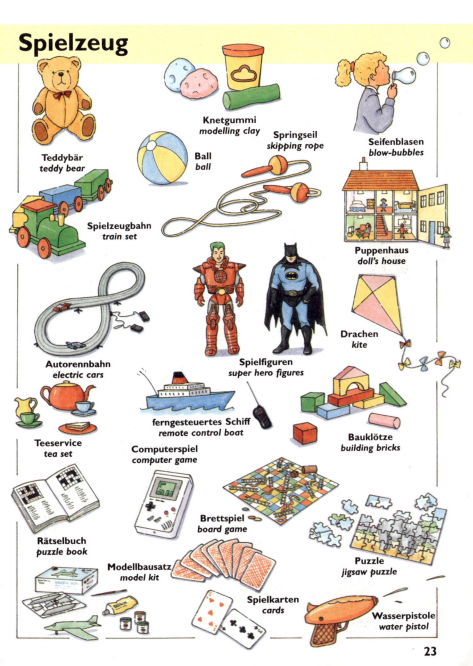

In der Schule

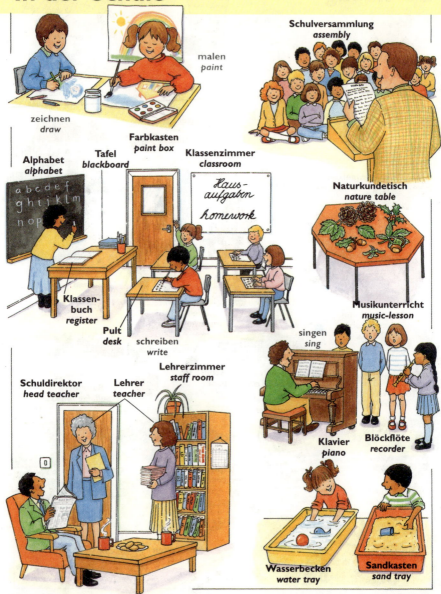

Formen und Farben

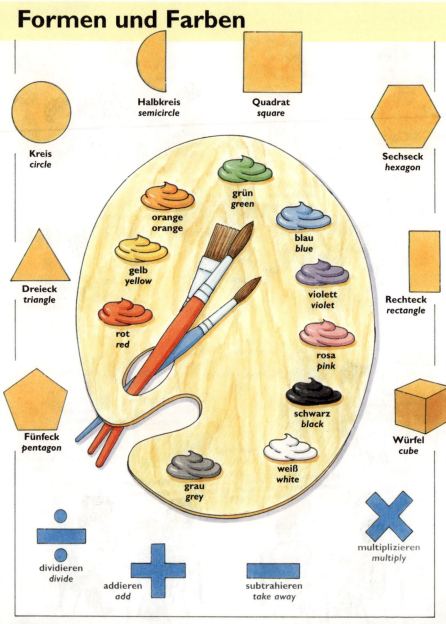

Märchen und Sagen

Unsere Erde

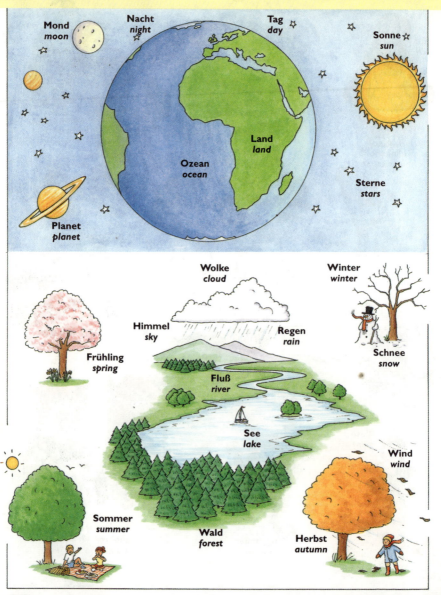

Wörterverzeichnis von A-Z

A

Aal 4
eel

Abfallkorb 12
litter bin

abladen 11
unload

abschmecken 15
taste

abwiegen 15
weigh

Achterbahn 7
roller coaster

addieren 26
add

Affe 4
monkey

alt 18
old

älter 18
older

am ältesten 18
oldest

Ameise 3
ant

Ampel 12
traffic lights

Anorak 22
anorak

Anrufbeantworter 17
answerphone

Arznei 21
medicine

Arzthelferin 21
doctor's assistant

aufwachen 16
wake up

Auge 20
eye

ausrollen 15
roll

Ausstechform 15
pastry cutter

ausziehen 22
undress

Auto 11
car

Auto fahren 11
drive

Autofahrer 11
driver

Autorennbahn 23
electric cars

B

Baby 18
baby

Bach 5
stream

Backblech 15
baking tray

Backofen 15
oven

Bäcker 13
baker

Badewanne 17
bath

Badezimmer 17
bathroom

Bagger 10
digger

Bahnhof 11
railway station

balancieren 25
balance

Ball 23
ball

Bank 12
bank

Bank 25
bench

Baseballmütze 22
baseball cap

Basketball 6
basketball

Bauch 20
stomach

Bauchschmerzen 21
tummy ache

Bauer 5
farmer

Bauernhof 5
farm

Bauklötze 23
building bricks

Baustelle 10
building site

Bauunternehmer 10
builder

Bein 20
leg

Besteck 16
cutlery

Beton 10
concrete

 Bruder 18
brother

 Computerspiel 23
computer game

 Eimer 8
bucket

 Bett 16
bed

 Buch 25
book

 Cousin 18
cousin

 Einkaufswagen 14
trolley

 Bibliothek 13
library

 Buchhandlung 13
bookshop

D

 Eis 8
ice cream

 Bienenstock 3
beehive

 Bulldozer 10
bulldozer

 Dach 10
roof

 Eisbär 4
polar bear

 blasen 19
blow

 Bungalow 10
bungalow

 Dachziegel 10
roof tiles

 Elefant 4
elephant

 Blattlaus 3
woodlouse

 Bürgersteig 12
pavement

 Dampfwalze 10
steamroller

 Elf 27
elf

 blau 26
blue

 Büro 10
office

 Daumen 20
thumb

 Ellbogen 20
elbow

 Blockflöte 24
recorder

 bürsten 17
brush

 Delikatessen 14
delicatessen

 Eltern 18
parents

 Boccia spielen 8
bowling

 Bus 11
bus

 Drachen 23
kite

 Enkel 18
grandchild

 Brettspiel 23
board game

 Bushaltestelle 12
bus stop

 Dreieck 26
triangle

 Ente 5
duck

 Briefkasten 12
letter box

C

 Drillinge 18
triplets

 Ententeich 5
duck pond

 Brot 14
bread

 Café 12
café

E

 entzündungshemmende Salbe 21
antiseptic cream

 Bruchsteine 10
stone slabs

 Computer 25
computer

 Eier 15
eggs

 Erde 3
earth

Erkältung 21
cold

 Fenster 10
window

 fliegen 11
fly

 Fußknöchel 20
ankle

 essen 19
eat

 ferngesteuertes Schiff 23
remote control boat

 Fliegenpilz 27
toadstool

G

 Etikett 14
label

 Fernsehantenne 12
TV aerial

 Flügel 3
wings

 gähnen 16
yawn

F

 Fernseher 17
television

 Flughafen 11
airport

 Gans 5
goose

 Fähre 11
ferry boat

 Feuerwache 13
fire station

 Flugzeug 11
aeroplane

 Garage 17
garage

 Fahrgäste 11
passengers

 Feuerwehrwagen 13
fire engine

 Flur 17
hall

 Garderobe 25
cloakroom

 fahren 11
drive

 Filzstifte 25
felt tips

 Fluß 28
river

 Garnele 9
shrimp

 fallen 6
fall

 Finger 20
fingers

 Flußpferd 4
hippopotamus

 Garnelennetz 9
shrimping net

 fangen 6
catch

 Fisch 2
fish

 Frosch 3
frog

 Garten 17
garden

 Farbkasten 24
paint box

 Fischernetz 3
fishing net

 Frühling 28
spring

 gebrochenes Bein 21
broken leg

 Federmappe 25
pencil case

 Fischfutter 2
fish food

 Fünfeck 26
pentagon

 Geburtstagstorte 19
birthday cake

 Fee 27
fairy

 Fleischer 13
butcher

 Fuß 20
foot

 gehen 2
walk

 Feld 5
field

 Fliege 3
fly

 Fußball 6
football

 Geisterbahn 7
ghost train

gelb 26 / yellow

 glücklich 19 / happy

 Hals 20 / neck

 Hecke 5 / hedge

 Geldautomat 12 / cash point

 Glückwunschkarten 19 / greeting cards

 Halsentzündung 21 / sore throat

 Heftpflaster 21 / sticking plaster

 Gemüse 14 / vegetables

 Go-Karts 7 / go-karts

 halten 2 / hold

 Heißluftballon 11 / hot air balloon

 Gemüsehändler 13 / greengrocer

 Goldfischglas 2 / fish bowl

 Hamburger 7 / burger

 Helm 6 / helmet

 Gepard 4 / cheetah

 Gorilla 4 / gorilla

 Hamster 2 / hamster

 Hemd 22 / shirt

 Gerüst 10 / scaffolding

 graben 8 / dig

 Hand 20 / hand

 Herzlichen Glückwunsch zum Geburtstag! 19 / Happy birthday!

 Geschenke 19 / presents

 grau 26 / grey

 Handgelenk 20 / wrist

 Hexe 27 / witch

 Geschirrschrank 16 / cupboard

 grün 26 / green

 Handschuh 22 / glove

 Hexenbesen 27 / broomstick

 Gezeitentümpel 9 / rock pool

 Gummistiefel 22 / rubber boots

 Handtuch 9 / towel

 Hexenkessel 27 / cauldron

 Gipsverband 21 / plaster cast

H

 Haus 10 / house

 Himmel 28 / sky

 Giraffe 4 / giraffe

 Haare 20 / hair

 Hausaufgaben 24 / homework

 Höhle 27 / cave

 Girlanden 19 / streamers

 Hai 4 / shark

 Haushaltswaren 14 / household items

 Holz 10 / wood

 Glocke 25 / bell

 Halbkreis 26 / semicircle

 Haustür 17 / front door

 Holzlöffel 15 / wooden spoon

32

Hose 22
trousers

 am jüngsten 18
youngest

 Kerzen 19
candles

 Klippe 9
cliff

 Hubschrauber 11
helicopter

 Juwelier 13
jeweller

 Kiesel 8
pebbles

 Knetgummi 23
modelling clay

 Hügel 5
hill

K

 Kino 12
cinema

 Knieschoner 6
pads

 Huhn 5
hen

 Käfer 3
beetle

 Kiosk 8
kiosk

 Knochen 2
bone

 Hundehütte 2
kennel

 Känguruh 4
kangaroo

 Kipplader 10
dumper truck

 kochen 15
cook

 Hüpfburg 7
bouncy castle

 Kaninchen 2
rabbit

 Kirche 13
church

 Kommode 16
chest of drawers

 hüpfen 6
skip

 Karussell 7
merry-go-round

 Klassenzimmer 24
classroom

 König 27
king

 Hut 22
hat

 Käse 14
cheese

 Klavier 24
piano

 Königin 27
queen

 Kasse 14
cash till

 Kleiderhaken 25
peg

 Konservendosen 14
tins

J

 Jeans 22
jeans

 Kassenbon 14
receipt

 Kleiderschrank 16
wardrobe

 Kopf 20
head

 Joghurt 14
yoghurt

 Kassiererin 14
shop assistant

 kleinschneiden 15
chop

 Kopfschmerzen 20
headache

 jung 18
young

 Kätzchen 2
kitten

 Klettergerüst 6
climbing frame

 Kopfsprung 9
header

 jünger 18
younger

 Katze 2
cat

 klettern 6
climb

 Korb 2
basket

Krake 4
octopus

 Küchenherd 16
kitchen stove

 Leib 20
body

 Mama 18
mummy

 Kran 10
crane

 Küchen-schrank 16
cupboard

 lesen 25
read

 Marienkäfer 3
ladybird

 Krankenhaus 13
hospital

 Küchenwaage 15
kitchen scales

 Lieferwagen 11
van

 Margarine 15
margarine

 kratzen 4
scratch

 Kuh 5
cow

 Liegestuhl 9
deck chair

 Mathematik 25
mathematics

 Kreis 26
circle

 Kühlschrank 16
fridge

 Lineal 25
ruler

 Maus 2
mouse

 Kreisverkehr 12
roundabout

L

 Löwe 4
lion

 Meer 9
sea

 Kreuzschiff 11
cruise liner

 Labyrinth 7
maze

 Luftballons 19
balloons

 Meerschwein-chen 2
guinea pig

 Kreuzung 12
crossroads

 Lamm 5
lamb

 Luftkissenboot 11
hovercraft

 Mehl 15
flour

 kriechen 3
crawl

 Land 28
land

 Lupe 3
magnifying glass

 Mikrowellen-herd 16
microwave oven

 Krokodil 4
crocodile

 Landhaus 10
cottage

M

 Milch 14
milk

 Krücken 21
crutches

 Lastwagen 5, 11
lorry oder truck

 machen 8
make

 Milchprodukte 14
dairy food

 Kuchen 14
cake

 Lehrer 24
teacher

 Mähdrescher 5
combine-harvester

 Modellbausatz 23
model kit

 Küche 16
kitchen

 Lehrer-zimmer 24
staff room

 malen 24
paint

 Mond 28
moon

Motorrad 11
motorbike

 Neffe 18
nephew

 Opa 18
grandpa

 Picknick 6
picnic

 Motte 3
moth

 Nest 3
nest

 Orange 26
orange

 Pier 8
pier

 Müllwagen 12
dustcart

 Nichte 18
niece

 Ozean 28
ocean

 Pinguin 4
penguin

 multiplizieren 26
multiply

 niesen 21
sneeze

P

 Pirat 27
pirate

 Mund 20
mouth

 Nudelholz 15
rolling pin

 Pantoffeln 22
slippers

 Plakat 12
advert

 Muscheln 9
shells

 Nudeln 14
pasta

 Papa 18
daddy

 Planet 28
planet

 Musikanlage 17
music system

O

 Parkhaus 12
multistorey car park

 Planschbecken 6
paddling pool

 Musikunter-richt 24
music-lesson

 Obst 14
fruit

 Pastete 15
pie

 planschen 8
paddle

N

 Obstgarten 5
orchard

 Patient 21
patient

 Plätzchen 15
biscuits

 Nacht 28
night

 Ohr 20
ear

 Pausenaufsicht 25
playground helper

 Po 20
bottom

 Nase 20
nose

 Oma 18
granny

 Pfannen-wender 15
spatula

 Polizeibeamter 13
police officer

 Nashorn 4
rhinoceros

 Omnibus 11
bus

 Pferd 5
horse

 Polizeifahrzeug 13
police car

 Naturkunde-tisch 24
nature table

 Onkel 18
uncle

 Pferdestall 5
stable

 Poller 12
bollards

Pommes frites 7
chips

 Popcorn 7
pop corn

 Postamt 13
post office

 Preis 19
prize

 Prinz 27
prince

 Prinzessin 27
princess

 Puderzucker 15
icing sugar

 Pullover 22
pullover

 Pult 24
desk

 Puzzle 23
jigsaw puzzle

Q

 Quadrat 26
square

R

 Radiergummi 25
rubber

 Rathaus 13
town hall

 Rätselbuch 23
puzzle book

 rauher Hals 21
sore throat

 Raupe 3
caterpillar

 Rechteck 26
rectangle

 Regale 14
shelves

 Regen 28
rain

 Reis 14
rice

 Reisebus 11
coach

 Rennboot 9
speed boat

 rennen 4
run

 Rennmaus 2
gerbil

 **Rettungs-
schwimmer** 8
life guard

 Rettungswagen 13
ambulance

 Rezept 15
recipe

 Riese 27
giant

 Riesenrad 7
big wheel

 Rinnstein 12
gutter

 Ritter 27
knight

 Robbe 4
seal

 Rock 22
skirt

 Rollbrett 6
skateboard

 Rollschuhe 6
roller boots

 rosa 26
pink

 rot 26
red

 Rotorblätter 11
rotor blades

 Rücken 20
back

 rudern 9
row

 rühren 15
stir

 Rührschüssel 15
mixing bowl

 Rutschbahn 6
slide

S

 Sägespäne 2
sawdust

 Sahne 14
cream

 Sand 8
sand

 Sandburg 8
sand-castle

 Sandkasten 24
sand tray

Satelliten-schüssel 12
satellite dish

 Schlauchboot 9
rubber dinghy

 Schülerlotse 12
lollipop person

 Schwimm-flossen 8
flippers

 satt 19
full up

 Schlinge 21
sling

 Schüssel/Napf 2
bowl

 Schwimmflügel 8
arm bands

 Schaf 5
sheep

 Schloß 27
palace

 Schulhof 25
playground

 Schwimmreifen 8
rubber ring

 Schal 22
scarf

 Schmetterling 3
butterfly

 Schulter 20
shoulder

 Sechseck 26
hexagon

 Schalter 16
switch

 Schnee 28
snow

 Schulversamm-lung 24
assembly

 See 28
lake

 Schatz 27
treasure

 Schnellimbiß 13
snack bar

 Schuppen 17
shed

 Seestern 8
starfish

 Schaukel 6
swing

 Schnitt 21
cut

 Schürze 15
apron

 Seetang 8
seaweed

 Schaumbad 17
bath foam

 Schnorchel 8
snorkel

 Schwarm 3
swarm

 Segelboot 11
sailing boat

 Schildkröte 4
turtle

 Schornstein 10
chimney

 schwarz 26
black

 segeln 11
sail

 schlafen 16
sleep

 schreiben 24
write

 Schwein 5
pig

 Seife 17
soap

 Schlafzimmer 16
bedroom

 schreien 7
scream

 Schweinestall 5
sty

 Seile 6
ropes

 Schläger 6
bat

 Schuhe 22
shoes

 Schwester 18
sister

 Sessel 17
armchair

 Schlange 4
snake

 Schuldirektor 24
head teacher

 schwimmen 9
swim

 Shorts 22
shorts

sich waschen 17 wash	Spielfiguren 23 super hero figures	Stethoskop 21 stethoscope	Surfbrett 9 surfboard
singen 24 sing	Spielkarten 23 cards	Stier 5 bull	Super-Rutsch-bahn 7 helter-skelter
Sitzstange 2 perch	Spielsalon 7 amusement arcade	Strandmatte 8 beach mat	Sweatshirt 22 sweatshirt
Sofa 17 sofa	Spielwaren-geschäft 13 toy shop	Straße 12 road	**T**
Sohn 18 son	Spinne 3 spider	Straßenbelag 10 tarmac	Tabletten 21 tablets
Sommer 28 summer	Spinnennetz 3 web	Straßenlaterne 12 lamp post	Tafel 24 blackboard
Sonne 28 sun	Spitzer 25 sharpener	streicheln 2 stroke	Tag 28 day
Sonnenbad 9 sunbath	Springseil 23 skipping rope	Strichcode 14 bar code	Tankstelle 12 petrol station
Sonnenöl 9 suntan lotion	Spüle 16 sink	Strickleiter 25 rope ladder	Tante 18 aunt
Spaten 8 spade	Stall 2 hutch	Stroh 2 straw	tanzen 19 dance
Spiegel 17 mirror	Startbahn 11 runway	Strümpfe 22 socks	Taschenkrebs 8 crab
spielen 19 play	Steige 5 stile	Strumpfhose 22 tights	tauchen 9 dive
Spielplatz 6 playground	Sterne 28 stars	subtrahieren 26 take away	Taucheranzug 8 wet suit

Taucherbrille 8 *goggles*

 Tisch 24 *table*

 Turnschuhe 22 *trainers*

W

 Taxi 11 *taxi*

 Toaster 16 *toaster*

U

 Wald 28 *forest oder wood*

 Teddybär 23 *teddy bear*

 Tochter 18 *daughter*

 Ungeheuer 27 *monster*

 Wand, Mauer 10 *wall*

 Teekanne 16 *teapot*

 Toilette 17 *toilet*

 Unterhemd 22 *vest*

 Warteschlange 7 *queue*

 Teeservice 23 *tea set*

 Tor 5 *gate*

 Unterhose 22 *pants*

 Wartezimmer 21 *waiting room*

 Teich 3 *pond*

 Torte 15 *cake*

V

 Waschbecken 17 *basin*

 Telefon 17 *telephone*

 Traktor 5 *tractor*

 Verband 21 *bandage*

 Waschmaschine 16 *washing machine*

 Theater 12 *theatre*

 Treppe 17 *stairs*

 Verkäuferin 14 *shop assistant*

 Wasserflasche 2 *water bottle*

 Thermometer 21 *thermometer*

 Treteimer 16 *pedal bin*

 Verkehrspolizist 12 *traffic warden*

 Wasserhahn 16 *tab*

 Thron 27 *throne*

 treten 6 *kick*

 Videorecorder 17 *video*

 Wassergraben 8 *moat*

 Tiefkühltruhe 16 *freezer*

 Troll 27 *troll*

 violett 26 *violet*

 Wasserkocher 16 *kettle*

 Tiefkühlkost 14 *frozen food*

 T-Shirt 22 *t-shirt*

 Vogelfutter 2 *birdseed*

 Wasserpistole 23 *water pistol*

 Tiger 4 *tiger*

 Tümpel 4 *pool*

 Wasserrutschbahn 7 *water chute*

Wasserschlacht 6
water fight

 Wohnungen 10
flats

 Zauberkünstler 19
magician

 Ziegelsteine 10
bricks

 Wasserschlitten 9
jet ski

 Wohnwagen 6
caravan

 Zauberer 27
wizard

 Zucker 15
sugar

 Wasserski 8
water ski

 Wohnzimmer 17
living room

 Zebra 4
zebra

 Zuckerwatte 7
candy floss

 weiß 26
white

 Wolke 28
cloud

 Zebrastreifen 12
zebra crossing

 Zug 11
train

 Wellensittich 2
budgerigar

 Würfel 26
cube

 Zehen 20
toes

 zuhören 17
listen

 Welpe 2
puppy

 Wurm 3
worm

 Zeitungshändler 13
newsagent

 Zunge 20
tongue

 werfen 6
throw

 Wurstbrötchen 7
hot dog

 Zelt 6
tent

 zuschauen 17
watch

 Wespe 3
wasp

 Zahnarzt 21
dentist

 Zeltplatz 6
campsite

 Zutaten 15
ingredients

 Wind 28
wind

 Zähne 20
teeth

 Zement 10
cement

 Zwillinge 18
twins

 Winter 28
winter

 Zapfsäulen 12
petrol pumps

 Zementmischer 10
cement mixer

Wissenschaftliche Beratung: Prof. Dr. Reinhold Freudenstein
Gründungsmitglied des Fördervereins »Kinder lernen europäische Sprachen«

Die englische Originalausgabe erschien 1993 unter dem Titel *First Dictionary* bei Colour Library Books Ltd,
England
© 1993 Zigzag Publishing Ltd, England
All rights reserved
Konzeption: Tony Potter
Text: Alison Niblo, Janet De Saulles, Nicola Wright
Beratung: Betty Root
Gestaltung: Kate Buxton

Für die deutsche Ausgabe:
© Delphin Verlag GmbH
in der VEMAG Verlags- und Medien Aktiengesellschaft, Köln
Alle Rechte vorbehalten
Printed in Italy
ISBN 3-7735-5678-0